Contents

Frogspawn

Something is floating on the edge of the pond. It looks like jelly with spots! It is thousands of tiny frogs' eggs, called **frogspawn**.

frogspawn

4

From Tadpole to Frog

Sally Hewitt

First published in the UK in 2014 by:
QED Publishing
A Quarto Group Company
The Old Brewery
6 Blundell Street
London N7 9BH

www.qed-publishing.co.uk

Designed by Melissa Alaverdy

A catalogue record for this book is available
from the British Library.

ISBN 978 1 78171 547 5

Printed in China

Picture credits

Key: t = top, b = bottom, m = middle, l = left,
r = right

Alamy 2-3 © Derek Croucher / Alamy, 17t © SuperStock /
Alamy, 19c © Jason Lindsey / Alamy, 22-23 © West Fine Art
/ Alamy

Ardea 8c Photographer © Brian Bevan / ardea.com, 13 br ©
John Daniels / ardea.com, 16b © Brian Bevan / ardea.com,
18l © John Daniels / ardea.com

Corbis 12b Thomas Marent

David Kuhn 20-21 ©David Kuhn/Dwight Kuhn
Photography

Ecoscene 8-9 Robert Pickett, 12-13 Robert Picket

FLPA 4-5b Roger Tidman/FLPA RM, 5 Derek Middleton/
FLPA, Derek Middleton/FLPA, 7b Alwyn J Roberts/FLPA,
7t Foto Natura Stock 7t, 10-11 Derek Middleton/FLPA,
12 Dave Pressland/FLPA, 23tr Roger Tidman/FLPA RM

Getty 14l Stephen Dalton

Nature Photo Library 1 Jane Burton, 14-15b Stephen
Dalton

Photolibrary.com 11r Oxford Scientific

Shutterstock 3 tristan tan, 4-5t Potapov Alexander, 7
Tshooter, 8 Emir Simsek, 14t Menno Schaefer, 14-15t
Aleksandr Sulga, 16-17 Shane Gross, 18 © John
Daniels / ardea.com, 19 Hein Nouwens, 24 Aleksandr
Sulga, 24 bl TSpider

Words in **bold** can be found in the Glossary on page 24.

Ten days go by. The sun
warms the eggs.

The little black dots
grow bigger and start
changing shape.

Tadpoles

Tiny **tadpoles** wriggle out of the jelly and swim away. They have big heads and long tails.

The tadpoles eat water plants.

A big fish in the pond watches the little tadpoles.

Big fish eat little tadpoles!

Breathing Underwater

gills

Young tadpoles stay underwater all the time. They breathe through **gills** on the side of their head.

But tadpoles keep changing!
After four weeks they start
breathing through new gills
inside their body.

Froglets

When they are eight weeks old, the tadpoles grow two back legs.

Now the tadpoles swim to the surface to take gulps of air.

A few weeks later, the tadpoles grow front legs too.

Their tails slowly disappear.

The tadpoles have become little frogs, called **froglets**.

They have long back legs for hopping and **webbed feet** for swimming.

Water and land

Froglets swim in the pond and sit on stones, floating leaves and lily pads.

They hop around on land
and hide in long grass.

Raccoons, skunks, snakes, turtles and birds all feed on frogs. But little speckled frogs are hard to see in the grass.

Frogs

All summer,
the little
frogs eat and
eat and grow
and grow.
There is plenty
of food around.

In autumn, the leaves start to drop from the trees and it begins to get colder.

There is not as much food for the young frogs now.

Winter and spring

The frogs find a hiding place in piles of leaves or under logs.

They sleep through the cold winter.

Spring comes and the frogs wake up. The male croaks to attract a female.

Now there is a new clump of frogspawn on the edge of the pond.

Glossary

froglet a baby frog that looks just like a grown-up frog

frogspawn a clump of thousands of frogs' eggs, each surrounded by a jelly-like substance

gills the parts of a tadpole's body that are used to breathe underwater

tadpoles small, black fishlike creatures that change into frogs

webbed feet feet are webbed when the toes are joined together by pieces of skin